MW00627190

The Best Little Girl Says Good-Bye

The Best Little Girl Says Good-Bye

A Therapist Grieves

Blanche Rosen Goodwin

Rutledge Books, Inc.   Bethel, CT

Rutledge Books, Inc.
8 F.J. Clarke Circle, Bethel, CT 06801

Manufactured in the United States of America

Cataloging in Publication Data
Goodwin, Blanche Rosen.
  The best little girl says good-bye : a therapist
grieves / Blanche Rosen Goodwin.
      p. cm.
      ISBN 1-887750-30-4
      1. Suicide.   2. Parents--Death--Psychological
aspects.   3. Adult children--Psychology. I. Title.

155.937--dc20   96-69978

Dedicated to my mother
Hilda Epstein Rosen
1913-1942
.... and all who journey to seek peace with loss

In 1982, during my training as a family therapist at The Family Institute, in Mt. Vernon, New York, I became aware of the many cut-offs that followed my mother's death. Over the following four years, I began a search to find family members and reconnect to my mother's two sisters and their families.

The reunions that followed were poignant and wonderful. For a period of time this sustained me. We shared photos, letters, tears and stories. It was a mix of the joy of discovery and the pain of knowing forty years had passed, some of which we simply could not recapture.

What began as an "educational" task had become an intense emotional process. The family messages I received as a little five year old and in the years following the loss of my mother were being reiterated. Pretending not to be in pain or sharing our feelings became the way our family remained "okay." I learned to repress all of my pain and protect everyone around me. I was now taking care of myself, re-experiencing old pain, letting it go.

I used journal and letter writing as my tools for this period. They allowed me to speak in the first person. A general theme like loss became personalized. My journal also created dialogue and conversation. It committed my emotions to paper. From the "fact" of the situation I moved to the emotional experience. The feelings came to the surface as I wrote and then read aloud. It connected an event like my mother's suicide to its impact.

I'm in kindergarten. It's snack time—milk and cookies. I can hardly wait. Peanut butter cookies in a big metal tin. Mr. Goldberg, the cookie-man, delivers them to our school. He's a short, smiling, chubby man with a big mole on his chin.

The teacher, Mrs. Syracuse, wearing a flowered smock, begins to hand out the cookies. I reach for one, and she says, "You didn't bring your money in on time. Wait until everyone is served and if there are extras I'll be back."

I wait and wait. She returns with crumbs at the bottom of the can. A sad, sad, shameful feeling comes over me. If I had a mom, my money would be in on time. The shame is, I'm different. I can't swallow the crumbs as a little tear rolls down my cheek.

"**H**ilda-a, Hil-d-a-a, where are you?"
Those screams from my dad are to change my life forever. I see him looking in my room. It's a dark cold January night. I follow him downstairs. I stand frozen at the kitchen door as I watch Dad carry Mom into the living room. I can't remember the next moments other than the chaos of neighbors running, screams, people in bathrobes. My mom has committed suicide by carbon monoxide asphyxiation.

In that one moment of peering through our screen door onto the darkened driveway, I was transformed from a carefree, smiling five year old with blonde curls to adulthood.

After my mother's death, relatives on both sides of the family distanced themselves and then eventually cut-off contact from one another for years. Each side has difficulty understanding why. Was it my dad's attempt to begin a new life? Was it hurt feelings because my mother's family took a new place of lesser centrality?

As a good daughter, I bought the party line and kept the distance. Loyalty seemed to mean no contact. I think it's safe to assume that the real reason for the separation was the pain of my mother's death, the shame of the suicide, and the step-family that formed three years later. In the early 1940s, little work was done to help families make transitions.

Once during a high school job in the summer of 1952, I met a biological cousin and an aunt. I couldn't handle the feelings of disappointment they expressed at not having seen us for so long. They were angry. I was frightened and fled.

3

In 1982, I began a search that reconnected me to my biological family. My step-family was very loving—still is—but I was not complete.

I am a "survivor" of a suicide. Of course we didn't "lie. " We just pretended. We just didn't talk of another life or any pain. It wasn't permitted.

We all operated with an extreme sense of denial by pretending to be a biological family—the "Brady Bunch," Long Island-style.

My Dad feared upsetting my step-mother. The word "step-mother" was thought to be a negative, awful put-down, like the wicked step-mother in Cinderella.

Over the years, photos of my mom were given to me by dad in hallways and coat closets of restaurants.

This process did not begin on the evening I sat in the T.O.F.[1] group receiving coaching. On the way to that group I could physically feel a tremendous well of sadness coming up in my throat. I looked out of the car window and saw the bright sky. It seemed like a good sign.

My trip through this period included the weaving together of different therapies. In the past, I had presented my three-generational family history, or "genogram," and my mom's suicide as "facts" in the most intellectual way. I was so out of touch with feelings. It wasn't safe until recently to dare to find them. A good kid wouldn't let out the family secret. I was taught in cruel ways that feelings were unacceptable.

I am now rewriting my definition of being "healthy" or "together." It seems okay to be open, though scared. The price of silence was simply too much. The "best little girl" had to take care or herself this time. Holding on to sadness quietly and privately, holding in anger, not dealing with conflict and presenting myself as "up," were no longer working.

---

[1](Therapist's Own Family). A T.O.F. Group is one in which a therapist can work with supervision on her own family-of-origin issues)

In order to move ahead, I had to clear the past. I needed to formulate and trust my new definitions. I had to stop waiting for the people around me to "understand." I had to get out of my head and into my heart. And amazingly, my head works better when I trust my heart. My heart was telling me to reach toward my mother.

I had never said good-bye. The group helped me in my decision to formally mourn my mother. I needed to work on this on an emotional level.

This time I would take a giant step. I would go "public" with my mother's suicide and my own grief. Our blended family would soon feel quakes.

I would be the one to open up a secret that had been held for 44 years. Much of my old way of being defined was to be so good. I took better care of my dad's need to keep the secret than my own need to "let it out."

I visited my rabbi and asked him to perform a second funeral with all the prayers and ritual that had been denied me. In his effort to protect me he attempted to talk me out of doing this. "Haven't you suffered enough?" he asked. I answered, "I have suffered more by not going through the feelings." I am strong enough now to experience the pain. I had to remain firm as he became one more adult that said, "go around the feelings." I told him, "I have already decided to do this. Will you as my rabbi help me?" In the days ahead, his presence was a great comfort.

The following letter to my friends and family was my invitation to them to join me for the mourning period following the funeral.

April 8, 1986

In January 1942, my mother Hilda Rosen took her life. I was five years old.

At that time, as their way of protecting and loving me, my family sealed over that tragedy and I never mourned her loss.

Those of you close to me know that I've opened up that chapter of my life, found relatives I've been cut off from, and have begun to learn who my mother was. In working on myself, I can now be open to my sadness.

As part of that process, I have chosen to formally observe Shiva at my home on the following days:

*   *Thursday, April 17th from 2 p.m.*
*   *Friday, April 18th from 2 p.m. to sundown*
*   *Saturday, April 19th from 2 p.m.*
*   *Sunday, April 20th from 2 p.m.*

Please join and help support me during this period.

Blanche Goodwin

Observing a mourning period was the ritual I chose to enact my mourning and grief. It offered me a way to try new roles like being open, sad, dependent, helpless, vulnerable. Evan Imber Black describes how ritual helps us get through transitions in her book, *Rituals in Families and Family Therapy*.

Wearing a cut black ribbon, participating in the funeral service, receiving visitors and saying prayers at the nightly religious service at my home gave a formality and credibility to the process.

The ritual allowed both Mom's life and her death to be brought out. I had wonderful photos to share. I could now show people who she was. A photo of her on the beach as a young woman. Her short curly hair, full figure and expression bearing a striking resemblance to my daughter Barbara.

Another of her wedding. A regal, breathtaking pose in her tiara and cream colored satin gown, draped in folds. Yet another of her holding my twin brother and I, looking so proud in a print dress with a lace collar. The quintessential feminine woman.

My step-mother was unprepared for my openness, though my biological mother was one of her best friends. She felt she had failed as a substitute if I needed to mourn. "I thought if I was a good mother you would never do this!" She was following the culturally prescribed role of a woman who could be everything.

It has taken us three and a half years to work through this relationship. Recently, I was able to thank her for being such a constant force in my life. She has come far as I continue my search. Her fear that I would abandon her by this search was not realized.

My step-sister was upset. "Couldn't you have done this privately?" she asked. She was only following the family rules of secrecy. She feared my grieving would create pain for my step-mom, and perhaps for her.

What I was unable to say then was, "I need to do this openly because suicide victims like my mom lose their past." The act itself is so unacceptable to society that silence becomes the punishment. In the last century, whole families were run out of their towns as a consequence of having a relative take their own life.

If my mom had died in another, socially acceptable way, I could have grieved normally. Silence and avoidance prevailed. I lost my beautiful, vibrant, 28 year old mom, and all of her history was sealed at that moment. Her legacy was pain, shame and denial.

Not being reactive was very important during this grieving period. Allowing the people around me to have their opinions, yet doing what I needed to do. Not attacking them, not needing their approval. Just simply staying with my task and remembering this was for me. There is no way to take care of yourself and please everyone else.

I did that for so long. The price was enormous self-denial and the repression of my feelings. Also, understanding that the way I was proceeding was unusual. The people around me were simply doing more of what we were used to, protecting in their way, not feeling, intellectualizing. I couldn't expect them to be where I was, and I couldn't wait for the "right time"—that time was now—so I continued the process.

The first big step after joining the T.O.F. group was writing a letter to my mom as if she could actually hear it. This would be one of a number of conversations we would have.

I sign it with a nickname given to me at birth by our nurse... Nurse Thompson. She called me "Peachy" and it stuck, as did "Buddy" for my twin brother Norman.

The letter I wrote to my mom to be read at the cemetery flowed just as my tears did. Now was the time. I could wait no longer. I could not talk myself out of feeling. I was ready to take care of myself in this way.

Lynn Anderson speaks in her book *Crystal Woman* of a child who grows up "minding" her parents and always fearful of their reactions as she learns to control her environment as a way of surviving. I was such a respectful child, not talking about my mom's suicide. It was my feelings that I learned to control.

1935 Mom's wedding pho

1936 Mom and her twins,
Peachy and Buddy

March 3, 1986

Dear Mom,

I've brought some of the family with me today, my husband Phil, my son Steven, my daughter Amy, Dad and Terry, Rabbi Lantz. I'm doing an unusual thing. I am going back in time and taking whatever time it takes to mourn your death.

To many people around me, even the ones who love and care for me, this mourning period seems bizarre or slightly gimmicky. To many it looks as if I've chosen four days of Shiva to have my quick catharsis. What I'm doing is part of a very long process of working on myself.

It's only because of years of hard work, often alone, that I have the strength to know and trust I can open that sadness and come out whole. Though I've asked many people to join me in the coming days, I know in some ways they may never understand what I'm doing.

They have only to be with me. I've learned over the years to do many unpopular things if I believe in them. When I visited you last time, I could barely contain my grief. I received many messages along the way to push that grief down.

I've had wonderful guides take me through this process. It's not a quick process. I am persistent, courageous, strong, committed to having the best life and discovering all the parts of myself.

It's often a lonely process, sometimes frightening. I go deeper and higher. I have such sadness that you missed this opportunity to live out a full life. It's not a trip in despair at all. The despair sets in only when the process gets bogged down or stuck, when I fight it, or push away the people who love me.

I'm daring now to challenge my husband Phil—to trust him

more, to let him see the sad part of me and to allow him to do more—because right now I need to take care of myself. One area of fallout has been doing for others and not letting anyone in very far. Losing you was so profound, I overdeveloped my competence and learned not to need anyone.

It feels as if I've held onto that sadness for so long. Maybe for as long as you paced the tan linoleum kitchen floor. I saw you and hid behind the door. That little space became my haven as even at five I did not miss much.

Then the night you took your life Dad screamed so loudly I responded. There I was at the back door standing helplessly. You lay motionless in the driveway, having found your peace.

I was a very good girl and the messages were clear. I was hearing "you are the strong one." I told the kids on the street exactly what Dad told me to say. "My mom went to Florida." Of course they knew it was a lie. Every neighbor ran out into the January blackness.

It was like a holocaust. I remember thinking this was the air raid we prepared for in school. Why else would everyone be at our house in the middle of the night? But I did not question. I attempted at times to take care of Dad and Buddy and later Louise. My brother remembers comforting me on the staircase as the doctor tended to our already dead mother. I was in shock and couldn't take it in.

I learned from Dad you showed no signs of sadness the night of your death. You gave Artie the night off, cooked dinner for all of us... including Grandpa Rosen. You took your rings off prior to going to sleep and then in the middle of the night went out to the garage silently and ended your life.

I know now that I can be strong and vulnerable. They are not incompatible states.

I have so many unanswered questions. Why would a beautiful young woman and mother of twins leave us?

What was your relationship with Dad like? Few answers. Everyone assures me you two were in love. Was it your relationship with your parents and step-siblings that depressed you? Or did you have a physiological depression with no medication to address it? At times, I feel everyone protects me from information they might know.

Was it the jealousy of your step siblings with you being the only biological child of your parents. I learned there were many fights over jewelry and you being left at your father's home.

I've gone back to 179th Street and stood in front of the brown and white tudor house. The driveway that cradled your limp body barely looks big enough to hold anyone. The area is still one of pride. I've reconnected with your best friend Lee, and she's been great to me. At 80, she too harbors helpless feelings, "If only I came back to our friendship sooner. Maybe Hilda would be here." We grieved together in Florida, and see one another periodically.

I know I've repressed a lot of memories. I'm often only left with that night, the alley, the car running, your dead body in the living room. Guests who brought me presents—hankies with days of the week embroidered on them. I had no tears then as I was in shock.

I miss you Mom. Never to have watched me grow up, marry, have children. How did that handsome couple, on the beach with two beautiful kids have such a fate?

It's no accident that I gravitated toward a career in family therapy. It taught me to go back and reconnect in a family fraught with cut-offs. Dad marrying Terry provided us with the safety net of a loving and warm family.

Your sisters, Dottie and Essie, are speaking again after a 14-year lapse. Jack and Harvey (their sons) haven't spoken in over thirty-

five years. Cousins who live within a half hour of one another and carry the struggles of their mothers. Each cannot remember where it all started. Jack attempted a visit to Harvey, but Harvey was dying. His visit would be at Harvey's funeral.

I spent time with cousin Stanley in Tucson, Arizona.

I've visited Roslyn and her family following a call to her in December of 1984. I needed to persist in seeing her as she too was caught up in whatever cut us all off. The visit went quite well. Aunt Dottie went from an observing silence to giving me eye contact and a wonderful smile as she said, "I never thought I'd live to see this day." Tears came down her cheeks. She had me fooled all day into thinking she was senile. She's frail and in her late 80s.

That was to be my last visit with Roslyn. She died of kidney failure several months later. I'm so glad to have met her. We had made one other attempt when I was 16 but neither of us knew how to handle the visit. Her death brought her brother Jack and his lovely family nearer to me.

Buddy and I were so close but after Dad remarried we grew distant. I have been the apple of Dad's eye. I love him though he's a tough man. He was a dad who provided us with a smooth household in a neighborhood where I had lots of friends. He was also brutally punitive if I showed any emotion following your death.

I thought Artie was my mother for awhile and then Aunt Helen. They both left with no good-byes. Losing three significant women by eight years old set the stage for later problems with separation.

The good part of all these changes was that I now have the ability to get along with most everyone. I tuned into school early on— Buddy to subjects and me to the system and people. In no time at all I was class president, teacher's pet, monitor.

Terry has been the best stepmother anyone could possibly want.

She is loving and almost too giving. She caters to dad and loves me.

I'm almost fifty now and I have the luxury and urgency to deal with a lot of pain. I've been a successful mother, a good wife, a successful career woman, a good daughter-in-law. All of these roles have been demanding. I've balanced and re-balanced and done enormously difficult work to "do it all." I was losing myself by not doing this grief work.

We've seen Harvey and Ruth many times in the past two and a half years. They are fine, educated people. Harvey remembers adoring you in high school, and described you as a skilled swimmer.

Aunt Essie and Uncle Gus have been here and I there. They greet me so warmly when I call, and visit though they are quite elderly. Aunt Essie remembers taking you as a teenager to have your hair straightened... at Nick and Novella in N.Y.C. She also remembers taking you "to a doctor" four days before your suicide and seeing how tearful you were when the doctor asked if you might hurt yourself. He was not a psychiatrist and told Essie you might be in premature menopause. You kept telling the doctor you were sad.

How awful antidepressants were not available to you. You must have felt so alone and helpless.

Dad sees Helen and Belle but they are three people who have a great difficulty nurturing one another. Their role models for nurturing were short lived. Each was thrust into adulthood far too early.

I've learned some things about you from visits to relatives and photos. You were beautiful, athletic, elegant, a wonderful cook and manager, and a devoted mother.

My search even took me to a psychic who told me you liked music. She saw sadness in your photos of 1941, behind the beautiful clothes and posture.

I have been to the cemetery a few times. I'll be back. Somehow because I had you for so little time letting you go is so hard. I'm struggling to finish this letter.

Perhaps I can now say good-bye and hold on to what I'm learning about you in my search.

I love you.

Peachy

Aunt Essie, Mom
Aunt Dottie, Buddy
and Peachy

Mom, Dad, Buddy
and Peachy

I read the letter to my mom at her graveside and was aware of old familiar pulls. Take care of everyone else. They looked sad. All the words I had never dared to speak came out. I let people take care of one another while I leaned on my husband. I focused on the rabbi as he recited the prayers and pinned the traditional cut black ribbon on me. I watched my son take care of my stepmother. It was hard for me to read as my tears stained the pages and words became faint.

We returned home where friends had prepared a luncheon. In the following days, other friends, colleagues and family members arrived to pay their respects and comfort me. My moods swung from the joy of publicly showing them my wonderful album of my mom and the relatives I had found to the depths of despair as the reality and finality set in.

One bag of memorabilia said it all. In it were her birth and death certificates, golf permit of '41 and *The New York Times* obituary on torn, yellowed newsprint from January 21, 1942.

Some months later at my temple I placed a plaque on the wall of memory. It bears my mother's name, Hilda Epstein Rosen, and the date of her birth and death. This is another way of bringing her memory alive.

It is a symbol of her life and brief time with me. At 13, my twin brother Buddy was allowed to go to memorial services on the Jewish holiday of Yom Kippur. I was not.

Summer 1986

Dear Mom,

I haven't written to you since April when I visited your grave and mourned your death. At that time that very naive part of me probably thought, "Well, that's that." Now I've grieved.

Those few days were very special, very poignant, and so heavy. My back felt most of the pain. Friends gathered here at my home. I dared to be open, sending a letter out stating clearly that you had committed suicide, that I had to put that away to survive in the family and next in the step-family—that I had done a lot of work on myself and was now ready to face the sadness and pain of your death. Because it was so important, I asked people to help and support me, and they did.

Allowing people to see my vulnerability has been both difficult and rewarding. Since I was taught to hide sadness and be private, it was a mix for everyone.

Phil's support was tremendous. He's not a talker about issues, but he was there and he did not flee or pretend it wasn't happening. He stayed home for two days. Each of the children responded differently, but each personally to me, and each was with me.

Amy, my youngest, told me, "Mom, I never saw you cry." Imagine, superwoman not crying.

Steve, the oldest, following the funeral called me to say, "Mom, that was the saddest and most poignant day. You are an unbelievably brave woman." To Terry he said, "Grandma, I'm so lucky to have you. You're the only grandmother I've known."

Barbara, my middle child, had a delayed reaction as she was unable to attend the services. "Mom, this is too sad." She was able to let go of some of her own old agendas in the months ahead as a result of modeling my letting go.

I'm learning that my "doing" seals my "being." It's a form of running as I often never process or allow myself to get into what gets stirred up.

So what's been stirred up? I'm in a new position in the family. Some of it is my wish, and a differentiation step. Center stage, I found out, is simply too much. Moving from it has allowed Phil in more. I'm more a wife than a daughter now. Psychologically I took on Dad, some of it out of fear, some of it was out of sadness for him. I thought I'd fill in for you, never knowing it was impossible, always seduced by expressions like "you are my life." But all that is mostly intellectual. I have at times felt very lost and very alone.

I am more aware than ever that your presence and absence in my life was so important. The pain is there, few people to share this with. I've gotten incredible statements from people like, "Why now?" "Why at 50 do you have to do this?" "Well, was it worth it?" and "What new info did you find out?" They are very naive. At first I spent weeks explaining so they'd understand. Now I know they never will. I'm the only one who has to understand, or trust the process.

Some of my pain has to do with my getting connected to cousin Harvey who is dying of stomach cancer. I was able to sit with him and silently share his pain as I held his hand and stroked his brow. Politics everywhere. Making new connections so late in life only to find that I am soon to lose another cousin. Illness and frailty prevail. I'm proud of myself as I rarely run away from pain. I know my colleagues would say I have to learn not to run into it full speed.

I'll be writing again as it is of some comfort to now believe I can write even if I can't be with you.

Love,
Peachy

Through grieving my mother's loss and finding my biological family I have also reconnected to my dad's sisters, Helen and Belle.

This gave me a chance to thank Aunt Helen who moved into our house after my mom died. I've written her letters and visited her in Florida twice. We celebrated her 80th birthday together. We caught up on lots of past family history as we got reacquainted.

I no longer wait for opportunities, I create them.

Separations and losses stir up my sadness. Annie Bell, my housekeeper of twenty-nine years, retires and moves away. That old "loss" button gets pushed. The sadness, which until recently I could mask, simply overwhelms me. This time I don't push it down.

I'm less afraid of my own vulnerability. Sadness is one of my shades. It's part of who I am. Annie Bell opens her arms and I sob uncontrollably. A tiny, little lady who barely comes up to my shoulders holding me, a five-foot, six-inch woman.

This time seems different. I can allow someone else to take care of me. I can dare say this is hard for me—you took such good care of me. I also am reminded of another family housekeeper who lived with us from my birth until my mom's death, Artie. She died within 18 months of my mom.

Shortly after my dad remarried, Artie became ill and was hospitalized. I never saw her again or mourned her death. She was the central figure in our household.

23

As a way of going back, I wrote her a letter containing the words I wasn't given a chance to say. I have been so fortunate that Annie Bell and I keep finding ways to visit. We write, call and visit. For me, this significant woman in my life did not abandon me. She simply retired after years of dedicated service.

Dear Annie Bell,

There are so many feelings that I need to share with you at this time. First and foremost, you are ending the work part of our relationship with the same dedication and loyalty you've had for 29 years.

For me it is difficult because you are one of the few people I allowed to mother me. Little ways—an ice pack for a headache, a cup of tea. Big ways—taking care of my belongings.

Bigger ways—loving me and my children. In many ways we are alike. We complain little, we work so hard, we take life and work seriously. We push even if we're not well. Give us a job, we do it!

On another level altogether, you do and always will have a special place in my heart. You remind me of a person who also loved and cared for me when I was just a little girl. Her name was Artie. The difference is she left me and I never got a chance to even say good-bye or thank her.

I look forward to our continued relationship. I know we will seek one another out. It is now your turn to take care of yourself, and let others care for you.

You've put in so much. Thank you for being you and loving us so much.

Love,
Peach

I decided to put Artie's memory to rest.

March 9, 1987

Dear Artie,

I've been thinking of you over the past few years as I reconstruct the family, and very recently as my housekeeper, Annie Bell, retires and moves. Only now am I beginning to realize how much I needed to seal over, repress, not remember.

I'm getting a chance with Annie Bell I never got with you. To say good-bye. In the past, endings were with a person being there—one moment loving and caring for me, and then gone with no transition. Just ripped away, leaving my heart with a tear. Crazy isn't it?

First my mom whom you called "your baby" and loved so much. Then Aunt Helen, who helped us by moving in, and then you. How I wish you were here. I have so many questions which will go unanswered forever. What did you know about my mom that I can never know? What was she like before her depression?

I want to share the child fantasy part which gave me such comfort. You helped me construct a mini-world, after my mom died, and perhaps while she was alive. The basement where you washed and ironed was my favorite place. Buddy as the Lone Ranger and me as Tonto, and you right there. Little silly memories like chiclets, two in a box, a rabbit, a dog, cocktail franks on a string, always something you brought back from your day off.

Do you recall the "victory gardens" those rabbits destroyed? How about garbage trucks with cans to collect fat for the war.

I remember walking you to the bus stop and meeting you there after your return. I can't remember your illness though Terry tells me you had diabetes and high blood pressure. I can remember how scared you were when you knew dad would remarry. I was on your lap and you told me Terry was very smart but the air was ominous, and you transferred some fear about the future family.

I know it was the fear you'd be replaced as primary caretaker to us. I am putting together pieces of the past. I realized this weekend that my dad found it easier to put women in charge of pain, of feelings—you to take care of us and Hilda and Terry to visit you in the hospital. It blows my mind that dad did not visit you in the hospital or go to your funeral. And at the same time look at his past. He never said good-bye to his mom. She was taken away, following a depression at 28 years old. He never saw her again. Exactly the same age my mom was the time of her suicide.

He never said good-bye to my mom as she took her life. Perhaps losing you was too much. To this day he puts Terry on the phone to deal with the world. I grew up so quickly, coming out of that household. I took over the role of caretaking of my dad, and learned how not to say I had needs. I can "take charge" of anything, though I'm working hard to let others take care of me.

I just thought as I write to you that perhaps some of my good nurturing skills come from you. For our 50th birthday, I gave Buddy a wonderful print of the Cream of Wheat man talking to Aunt Jemima. She looks exactly as I remember you.

Remember Essie, Gus, Dottie and their kids? Well, I've found all of them after 45 years. We see one another, though they're elderly and unable to get around too much. A mix of feeling connected, yet time running out.

I've also gone back to 179th Street to look at our house. It looks tiny now. A neighborhood of tudor homes, on tiny lots, lawns neatly trimmed. At the time of my visit the trauma of helping Dad find Mom returned as I looked at the driveway.

Buddy and I have found one another again over the past 15 years. Remember all the wonderful kids on 179th Street. I could hardly wait to return from school. It was the warmest street imaginable. All the good memories of the playground on the corner and the bookbus that drove up each week and served as our library.

Thank you for taking care of Mom. I know now her death signaled yours. Thank you for loving us in millions of ways. The baby in me would love to recapture being cared for as you cared for me.

In many ways Annie Bell approached that—another fine, hardworking, giving woman.

I miss you.

Love,
Peachy

A letter to my step-mother, Terry:

July 25, 1987

Dear Mom,

I'm reflecting a bit on the day of my cousin Harvey's funeral. I wanted you to know you were and are simply super. You came willingly. You are so warm and helpful when someone is hurting. You are a lady.

I love you for all this and so much more. I continue to struggle and yet clear the past. The theme of loss is still profound for me. Losing him after such a short time and long cut-off, pulls at my heart.

Your strength and your own struggle with all of this have drawn us closer, not further apart.

Peach

In 1987, as I continued to clear difficult areas of my life, the courage I had to mourn my mother and find my biological family allowed me to challenge parts of my marriage. Once again, I scared those around me. The letter to my step-mother was not child to adult, but woman to woman. It followed a difficult, lonely time for me, yet a time of resolution and growth.

Letter to my step-mother, Terry:

February 23, 1988

Dear Mom,

Have a little time today and thought I'd put some feelings down that have been cooking.

Things here have turned a corner, and all the risks I dared to take in October have proven worthwhile. As that clears, I can once again get my energy for other areas of my life. I've been through hell and back again, as part of my struggle.

I haven't really told you in very long time how much I respect you. Many aspects of my search are baffling to those around me, as was the October "clearing" I needed to do and the way I chose to do it.

I have reconnected with cousins, aunts, children of cousins. That is settling in now. More parts of my life "picture" or "puzzle" are shaded and colored in. Though it was very painful for you, I needed to do that and still continue on that course. It's part of who I am.

Surely as a wife I know how "no win" our roles can be, especially if we take stands. And surely as a mother, I know how difficult the course can be. I know how outstanding you were and are, to have stepped into a new family and done such an incredibly good job.

Many things have changed in my life. Many roles have been redefined. Early trauma marked my young life. Changes from the 50s woman to the 80s woman continue to challenge me. But you have been a constant.

So, isn't it great to receive such a note and it isn't even Mother's Day or Valentine's Day? Just a day I am taking the time to say:

I love you.
Peachy

Dad takes me to his garden. He asks me to dig up a beautiful flowering plant when he dies. "It's a plant your mother planted in our first house. The plant is called a bleeding heart."

I'm beginning to say good-bye to my dad, to let him go, to open the subject of his failing health. I share with him how desperately I needed him as a little girl and how deep my connection is over time. I dare tell him how hard it will be for me when he dies. Soon I will dare to confront his abusiveness.

At my dad's 80th birthday celebration, my twin and his wife put together a collage of how our family really is, my biological mother, my step-mother, old photos and new, a blending of our histories. Our past is now incorporated as part of our history. This, plus our individual remarks as we toast him refering to the past and present, create a storm.

Discomfort arose and I receive a call from my stepsister after the celebration. "My family is tired of hearing about your mother. Promise me you'll never bring up her name !"

I reply, "There is no way I can promise you that. She is part of my history."

I recall my toast and tribute to my dad at that celebration.

December 1987

Dad's 80th Birthday

I'd like to share a few insights I've learned in the 50 years that I have known my dad.

Dad, you taught me:

* *To take risks, jump in and figure it out later.*
* *Not to be petty.*
* *To go ahead, and not be bitter about the past.*
* *To be a sport.*
* *To be independent, or as independent as a woman from the 50s could be.*
* *To be inquisitive intellectually.*
* *To be aware politically of other than my own ideas.*
* *To fight like hell for what I want.*
* *To be sure of myself even if my stance is unpopular.*
* *How systems work: Three generations of knowing how to come up with privileges.*

My favorite times, Dad:

* *A pony ride on the way to Rockaway.*
* *Chocolate Cat Tongues during WW II.*
* *Fleer's Double Bubble Gum you found for us when no one else could get it.*
* *A trip to the lower East Side where the gypsies strolled the streets.*
* *Rides you gave me and other kids when other Dads weren't available.*
* *Great love whenever you see me.*

My dad is a mix, like all of us. He had one sad, non-nurturing background. He can be tough. He can be opinionated. He can be stubborn. He can silently withdraw if he doesn't approve.

My dad is a survivor. He is not a complainer. He knew the Hyman family would give us love and warmth that his family was unable to, because they suffered so much early trauma and pain.

Will you join me and applauding my dad for his strengths and accepting his limitations?

The best little five-year-old couldn't possibly have her mom commit suicide. I remember being so tuned in to impending tragedy and doom that my only control was to mount a watch from behind a door.

My mom's anxiety became so unmanageable she paced our tiny linoleum floor staring downward. Over and over, back and forth, day after day. I was mesmerized by the rhythm. In my innocence I was sure if I watched hard enough she'd stop.

The naive part of me thought I had my catharsis in April 1986. I now know we have life issues and we chip away at them, bringing them closer to resolution. The child in me wishes the pain and sadness were gone forever.

My dad told me he was warned to mount his own watch. One night he fell asleep before my mom and when he awakened she was gone.

I am becoming clear and free of the past secrets, needing less approval, risking unpopularity, not waiting for or expecting people to understand, taking care of my needs, admitting my own vulnerability, acknowledging and feeling my own sadness, not fooling myself about feelings by rationalizing with family clichés like "count your blessings," daring to go through the iced-over feeling of "being left."

Sunday, November 13, 1988

While on tour of an area in Brooklyn called "Little Odessa," I realize I am quite near the neighborhood I was born in. Ocean Parkway and Ave. M. At the end of the day I see a sign over a storefront, it says "Reader." My husband and friends are apprehensive. I ask them to wait for me and I climb a long flight of steps.

The reader looks puzzled at one point. She says, "I see your mother is dead yet she is very much alive!" It is my search that has allowed her presence to live on in her photos, stories of her life, relatives I've found.

I am beginning to see turning points as new beginnings. In my earlier history, because of that early trauma, transition meant "the end" and emotional meant "death."

The search is what it's about, the process and not any specific information. We are fooled in our culture into believing that there is a goal of data.

In Lynn Andrew's *Star Woman*, she searches for a piece of art called a marriage basket. It is the search which leads to a personal transformation, and not acquiring the basket itself.

I hold back from turning in my manuscript. Something feels unfinished. It's so tidy. I'm unsure of what the something is. I'm in Florida in February of this year and as I'm writing, an old question surfaces from a very deep old place.

I decide to check out with my dad who is vacationing near by, whether I imagined being force-fed my own vomit when I could not swallow at mealtimes after my mom's suicide.

I wanted to hear that as a small child the threat was the reality and not the act. To my dismay, I learn he followed through on the threat. To my further dismay, my dad appears proud and comfortable as he tells me, "Yes, it happened. When I got through you never did that again!"

I am so accustomed to holding in old primitive feelings following my mom's loss that I get through our breakfast together and never react to his words. But my body reacts and every muscle pulls out in my lower back. I am humped over and tilted to one side. I cannot stand up straight. It will be a month before the pain leaves that area. The body never lies.

I go through the motions of the remainder of my vacation. The pain is excruciating. The coming months allow the rage, sadness and disappointment to surface. I will need to confront my dad when he returns to New York in April. I can no longer carry this burden. I need to be free of this pain. He needs to take responsibility for his inappropriate behavior. I need to show him the primitive sadness that swallowing my own pain masked.

Once again I have taken care of someone else and paid dearly. I begin by writing a letter to him and getting all my feelings down. I do not mail it. Instead I dare to let those feelings up. The helplessness I felt as a six-foot man stood over me, shoving vomit down my throat, the abuse of power he showed.

I tell my dad there is work for us to do. I need him to help me let go of this burden. I take this letter and bring it to my dad's house. At first he tries to change the subject. "Dad, today is my day for you to listen. Please don't respond quickly. Think about it all and I'll come back." I read it to him." He is defensive at first. "I was a good father, I did the best I could."

I reply that we are working on a particular piece of unacceptable behavior. I have always thought he was a good father in many ways—not in this way. I have shared this with him in the past, written about it and publicly toasted him on his 80th birthday. However, that does not excuse him. I need him to examine what he did—to look at it and take responsibility.

We need to go through the horror of his act and the words I never got to speak like, "Where is my mom?" "I miss her." "I'm so scared to have found her and seen her carried lifeless into our living room." "Why do I have to lie to my friends?"

I told my dad I want to work this through because I love myself enough now not to carry this pain. We will need to struggle through months of uncomfortable silences as I allow myself to feel and allow Dad to be sad. I am so good at taking care of him that my hardest task will be taking care of my own repressed feelings.

The family once again attempts to return to the status quo. My step-mother calls me and lets me know she is worried about my dad. "He's 83 and this may be too much for him."

My sister-in-law, Joan, seeing my dad one day and hearing him say I'm working on an old issue with him, also reacts by taking care of him. "Who picks up the pieces?" inferring I'll wreck something carelessly. My twin brother, knowing through my dad we are working on this, never once calls me to see how I'm doing. (In preparing the manuscript for publication, Joan shared her horror of learning of my dad's abuse of me. She was incredibly supportive recently. We just never took the time before now to talk about it.)

They are concerned about my dad, fearful of the feelings and attempting to seal it over. I persist in clearing this trauma and abuse.

I ask my twin, "Why is it I haven't heard from you? Even if you don't agree on the how, why didn't you ask if I was okay?" His answer is astounding. "I never think of you as having had a hard time with Dad. I thought of you as the favored one."

He then says he was wrong not to call to see if I was okay. I say to all of them, "Trust Dad and me to work this out. He is responding. It is painful. Trust our process."

My dad sent me a note...

I bring an audio cassette of a talk I delivered to the National Association of Suicidology about my journey in bringing closure to my delayed grief and finding out who my mom was and the where-abouts of her family.

I also write Dad a letter.

March 9, 1990

Dear Dad,

Florida was so similar to the way we proceeded as father and daughter in the 1940s. A sunny, happy together time. And some of it was paralleling and covering unspoken feelings.

I'm so happy that you and Terry spend winters at International Village. It seems to be the best possible environment for each of you. Some of the difficulties still remain, but most are a function of your ages and physical conditions.

When I was in Florida, I was revising my manuscript. I had written much of it in the same way our family presents—clean and tidy—I have worked through much pain resulting from Mom's suicide and the way in which the family chose not to deal with it emotionally.

One area has been surfacing that I need to clear with you specifically. That is the hideous punishment you forced upon me for my inability to swallow food following Mom's death. I know now it was all those feelings about her loss, the anxious months prior to her tragic ending, no place to share or deal with it.

How could I, a little five-year-old, eat in the same kitchen where I witnessed her unending pacing? How could I walk through the kitchen without remembering that night I watched you carry her into the house? I look at photos of myself and I was so cute, lively, animated before that time.

How could you have threatened me with putting my face in my own vomit? How could I swallow what was going on? I tried, God knows.

Until I discussed this episode with you in Florida, I had convinced myself that the threat never materialized and it was only the fear of pun-

ishment. But having asked you directly, "Dad did you feed me vomit?" and hearing you calmly reply, "Yes, and you didn't do that again," you seem so proud of your power. I've searched my memory and it's coming back to me now—I get that sick feeling—can't keep the food down. Aunt Helen counts, "Chew, chew, chew" to the beat and tells me to swallow. I'm sitting at the kitchen table under a towel rack that holds a strap you hung and Buddy was mostly threatened with. I was too good a kid for that.

So why is any of this important and where did it play out in my life over the years? Well, it taught me not to trust my own feelings. It was a lesson in intimidation.

I learned with you as a dad how to get around behavior like yours. Be silent, assume you did something wrong, not question, go into a dead stop, be diplomatic and too nice. Expect to be punished from significant people who love me. At times I'm simply over-compliant. Other times it churns and churns like vomit in my small body in 1942—and comes up like a volcano.

I am humiliated that my dad, who I love and took such good care of, could have done such a thing to me. I am ashamed of your behavior. I make excuses for you and other people who hurt me. I have a whole rationale involving your sad and punitive childhood that "explains it all." I am such an expert in understanding and perspective.

I am ashamed of that time in my life—though it is your behavior that is shameful. Between my mom threatening me with a knife or scissors for "touching" myself as she paced away, and you shoving vomit down my throat, it was hard not to blame myself, first for mom's death as the incidents were all so close—and I upset an already out of control person—then all the feelings of shame, confusion, hurt, loss come up and I'm forced to swallow them.

No wonder earlier in my life I had chronic sore throats and dry-heaves. No wonder I waited so long to confront Phil for issues not belonging to me.

Perhaps my tendency to "present" in a tidy way protects us from looking at that pain.

I am very angry at both your behavior and reaction to my bringing up the subject—I think you need to think about this and come back to me.

I need you to take the same good care of me on the inside as you did on the outside.

Peachy

SUNDAY, MAY, 13/1990

DEAR PEACHY.

    I HAVE BEEN, SAD AND
MISERABLE SINCE OUR LAST
CONVERSATION, ABOUT MY HANDLING
THE EATING PROBLEM,,NOT EATING.

    AT THE ADVICE OF THE
DOCTOR (HE WAS WORRIED YOU, LOOKED
THIN, AND DID NOT EAT, THAT YOU
MIGHT GET SICK)
    I DID NOT KNOW WHAT
TO DO, I REALIZE I DID NOT DO
THE RIGHT THING THEN, I DID
THE BEST THING, I KNEW. I AM
SAD. AND REGETFUL. THAT YOU DID
NOT TELL ME BEFORE AND WAITED
ALL THESE YEARS TO TELL ME AND
TRY TO STRAITEN THIS OUT WITH
ME. I DID AND DO LOVE YOU
VERY MUCH. AND ALWAYS WILL
I THANK YOU FOR GIVING ME

3 WONDERFUL, GREAT, BREAND ..
                CHILDREN
I ADORE, AND AM PROUD OF
WHAT, YOU ARE, DOING, AND
WHAT YOU ACCOMPLISED,
FORGET FORGIVE
         YOUR PROUD AND
   LOVING FATHER   MORRIS

Sunday, May 13, 1990

Dear Peachy,

I have been sad and miserable since our last conversation, about my handling the eating problem... not eating.

At the advice of the doctor (he was worried about you, looked thin, and did not eat, that you might get sick).

I did not know what to do. I realize I did not do the right thing then. I did the best thing I knew. I am sad, and regretful that you did not tell me before and waited all these years to tell me and try to straighten this out with me. I did and do love you very much and always will.

I thank you for giving me three wonderful, great, grandchildren I adore, and am proud of what you are doing and what you accomplished.

> *Forget, forgive.*
> *Your proud and loving father,*
> *Morris*

It will be this talk, these words, that get my own sadness going and help my dad move from punitive to repentant and ashamed of his behavior. We cry together. We plan a trip to the cemetery.

It is here (July 1990) before my mother's grave that we move through deep sadness to forgiveness.

I talk to my mom first, with my dad standing beside of me, his arm around me. I tell Mom that there was no place for me to be sad—that I held that sadness in my throat and chest and could not swallow. I tell her about the threats and finally the punishment. I am crying.

I tell her my dad did to me what was asked of him—repressed his own sadness—that intellectually I understand it. He didn't know how else to do it. But emotionally I've paid dearly. I tell her how sad I was to lose her and have no one to tell it to for fear of punishment.

My dad speaks next. "Hilda, I've done a terrible thing. If it is in your power to forgive me, please do so. Peachy needs to be free of this burden." He thanks her for giving him the first real home he had since he was a small boy. He tells her he is so sorry their marriage worked out the way it did—losing her to suicide.

He brags about how wonderful I am, how proud he is of me, all his children and grandchildren. We stand together, arm in arm, tears streaming down our faces.

We each place a pebble on her headstone which is neatly surrounded by ivy. He promises my mom he will do anything to help me through this—whatever it takes and however long it takes.

We walk away together in silence. One more time, I got through my own vulnerability. I did not flee. I did not attack. I did not stop doing what I needed to because others were anxious.

Today I was five again and my dad took care of me.

Dear Mom,

I'm writing to you today as I prepare to leave the Therapists Own Family (T.O.F.) group, a therapy group I joined in 1985 to assist me in bringing your suicide to a better resolution.

At that time, I had had a fair amount of therapy and three or four years of family therapy training. I was beginning to be aware that I had really not gone very deeply into your loss and my pain.

The group helped me narrow my scope and select tasks toward that goal. I never before depended upon a group for support. My position elsewhere which brought many goodies, much praise and an enormous price—to have everyone need me—that over-responsible position I have struggled long and hard with. I was about to reverse and balance that as I dared give that up and address my own needs, bring them to the surface—be vulnerable.

What I found here at T.O.F. was that it was okay to feel, to struggle, to be open about not having a perfect life. It became a safe haven. It was not simply safe in terms of venting. It was here that peers would question and confront, but not attack.

I want to share with you what is hard to leave. It is hard for me to leave Fredda Herz, Ph.D., Rob Goldberg, M.S.W. and Betty Widman, Ph.D.

I was blessed with colleagues that never judged me and always encouraged me to stay with my own process. I have had few such places in my life and perhaps I didn't allow it—or perhaps there are few such places. I took each one in as more than a professional colleague—I trusted each, I took each into my heart—I thought of it as another family—and it was.

I am sometimes wounded by my trust and openness, and this group was no exception. I got through one such wound from a short term member and was able to own that I try to fix things up or reach out—some people can't handle it and turn and attack.

I am entering a new stage in my life. Amy has left for college and for the first time in 30 or 32 years no children are home daily. At first I crashed. The 19 years of struggling to do a good job were over and I was initially focused upon what I gave up along the way and how hard I worked.

Actually, I love the peace and quiet as well as the visits. I love not being torn or split in my responsibilities. I also feel I gave Amy the best possible foundation an 18-year-old can have.

I'm sorting out whether "just my practice" will be enough, will be acceptable to me as an accomplishment. My work has never been better. I am deeply respected by my clients. All the human, feeling things I've done—especially since 1985—are coming full cycle.

I'd like to tell you about my colleagues and what was and is so special.

Our leader, Fredda Herz, Ph.D., has always treated me with great respect. She helped me move from wordy stories to stating what was going on and what I was struggling with—what did I need help with. Most of all—what is/was my part in any struggle. All of my experiences—student, supervisee—it is in the T.O.F. group where she shines and my respect and admiration deepened.

Betty and I had good chemistry from the start. It was her background, the magnitude of her losses, that allowed me to look at losing you and stop minimizing that loss. Her input has been invaluable, her friendship so precious.

Rob was always a man who could listen so well and say things only when they made a contribution. He sends as many caring messages with his presence or a look in his eyes. I always felt very cared for.

It was here too that I would go deeper and deeper. I never chose the quick way. I was very responsible to myself in the thorough way I dealt with unbelievably difficult work. My courage came up strongly. I am blessed with large doses of courage—even when I jump into the unknown.

I have formally mourned your death.

I have publicly acknowledged I am from a remarried family.

I have given up on the party line and trusted my own perceptions by finding your sisters and their families.

I have given up being popular in the family in the old way.

I have been open, honest and visible with my pain.

I have lived through the rejection, isolation and anger as people around me felt betrayed.

I have dared to confront parts of my marriage that were no longer working.

I have spoken at a national suicide convention.

More recently, following that talk, I was able to deal with Dad's punishments to me as a five-year-old as I attempted to feel your loss.

I have had enormous patience and persistence as it hasn't been smooth or simple.

I made time for this work and I honored the process.

I took the time to heal along the way and this is now who I am.

I've stood before your grave with Dad and got the chance to be five years old again and express five-year-old pain—50 years later.

I have given your life a dimension that earlier was buried.

As I read and write the list, I wonder how I did all this and still worked, mothered, wifed, and wrote on and on. No wonder I crash physically at times. More and more the crashes are time out, a spa. More and more I am accepting it is okay to nap or slow down.

I spend more time alone now. I need this time, can enjoy my own company, and do not necessarily feel lonesome.

Mom...

Your life and death, your relatives are more part of my general landscape. Earlier I was not allowed to say you were ever in the landscape at all. When I discovered you—your suicide, its impact, your life and its importance—you stuck out of the landscape—it's all blending now.

I sat with Steve at Yiskor services during Yom Kippur and shared with him that this holiday seemed lighter that the past four. He turned to me and said, "Mom, that's because you went through it and not around it." It was one of those special moments when I knew my journey impacted my son in the best way. Imagine turning a family secret, shrouded in shame into such a statement.

I am ready to move on in my life and that landscape. I hope to publish my story. I have done mega-work in T.O.F. I'm trusting my own internal message that the major work I entered to experience is over.

Having taken this journey I'm signing this letter with the beautiful name you gave me.

I love you Mom,
Blanche

I write this story for many reasons. The most important is for me. This is the story of the resolution of delayed grief. The process of this work and the struggles to go through it were deep and personal. This is a major clearing on my life's path. Yes, it was painful. Yes, it was wrought with conflict, turmoil, sadness and unpopularity.

But the pain of not doing it and the silence I kept was far worse. I attempted always to do it with dignity. It is my hope that reading it will give courage to others that it is "never too late" to deal with unresolved loss and grief.

Mom and Dad
c. 1940-1941

Buddy and Peachy

Mom and Buddy

Epilogue

July 19, 1996

I thought I might bring you, the reader, up to date on how recent events connect to the work described in the previous pages.

I realize now that I grew up with loss as a key issue. It is part of my fabric. I am finely tuned to it and knew early on the preciousness and precariousness of life... how transient... how temporar... a gift not to squander.

Since completing the manuscript for *The Best Little Girl*, my Dad has died. He was diagnosed with gastrointestinal cancer in June 1994 and his funeral was September first of that year. I held his hand as I told him he had less than three months to live. He was very brave and at peace. To lose my Mom to suicide and my Dad "with notice" was a new experience. This time I could say my farewells in person and be with him as he did a life review. He was 87 and mostly pleased. A metaphorical ledger he kept added up to more positives than negatives. He spoke of life in business terms. His children, their spouses, eight grandchildren, and Terry were his "assets."

The one area of angst was a cut-off started in Poland. He listened and got caught in the family turmoil and loyalty, ending a relationship with his maternal grandfather. He never forgave himself for this. The holocaust took charge and he never saw him again — or 17 other relatives. In many ways, his sharing this was a reminder that I went beyond the family script.

Dad lived until every last detail of his estate was in place. He and Terry had moved two years prior to a senior residence quite near my home. He left things in meticulous condition, providing the best quality of life for Terry. To this day, at 83 she is very well cared for, emotionally as well as physically, though it's hard for me as she has become so self-involved. I believe Dad wanted her to be cared for in every way as his way of thanking her for marrying him and helping him as they brought up their respective children.

I was able to give one of the eulogies at his funeral. I had a sense of calm and peace. It was real and balanced strengths and struggles.

This winter a former client, Larry, died of kidney disease and I spent some precious moments with him and his wife, June, hours before his death.

My favorite great uncle Dolph (from my step-family) died of lung cancer. In May of this year, my dear friend of 37 years, Sue, died and I spoke at her funeral. Without knowing our time together would be abruptly ended, we created time and space to love one another.

In June, Laura, a lovely 44-year-old client, died of an inoperable brain tumor. She and her husband, Jon, taught me so much about acceptance, spirituality, and the possibility of an afterlife.

I was part of the journey in each situation, as each made a special peace with life and death. The common thread was their bravery. I was able to open myself up to their pain, to the unknown. . . to trust my presence, my intuitions. . . to love each as they lost each physical battle.

I learned from each and the people around them, as I do from the many people I coach through all types of loss. It is a transactional process. To have more comfort about loss allows me to live more fully in the present. Of course when they cluster my body feels it and my heart went into tachycardia in May.

I was able to integrate the concept of being surrounded by the depths of pain and loss, yet at the same time recently celebrate my 60th birthday. I gave my twin brother a collage of photos from 1939 to 1941 he had never seen. The two of us on a beach looking so carefree... bottoms of bathing suits only. A photo of my mother holding my brother on that sunny day and beaming. Another taken later of my Dad and he playing in our yard. A third of my Mom leaning toward my Dad, arms around his waist, wearing a long print skirt, halter top, sandals, and, of course, her signature turban.

This time it wasn't sad. It was honoring a special time in our early childhood. I recaptured for my twin moments of our history that were lost and stored away when our tragedy struck. Over the course of writing my manuscript and sharing it with him, he spoke of the pain of our loss no longer as "frozen pain."

I've gone back to a traumatic time to re-experience and feel the hurt, betrayal, and pain denied me. I've reclaimed my silenced voice and in doing so gained new self-respect. We have few resources and little power as children to make choices about our own situations.

An early memory surfaces of my sitting on the floor of my bedroom in the first days following Mom's suicide. I was playing with my china dishes and pouring tea for my dolls as visitors found their way to my room to offer me comfort.

Geneen Roth's quote says it all:
"As for me, I am in the process of taking
my childhood room apart. And with each
memory of fear, each experience of loss,
the walls
are crumbling
and I am setting myself free."[1]

---

[1] Roth, Geneen. *When Food is Love.* Penguin Books USA Inc., New York, 1992.